T0037436

Oaths

Also by F.S. Yousaf

Euphoria

Sincerely

Prayers of My Youth

Serenity

Oaths

poems

F.S. YOUSAF

Andrews McMeel
PUBLISHING®

Oaths copyright © 2024 by F.S. Yousaf. All rights reserved.
Printed in China. No part of this book may be used or reproduced
in any manner whatsoever without written permission
except in the case of reprints in the context of reviews.

Andrews McMeel Publishing
a division of Andrews McMeel Universal
1130 Walnut Street, Kansas City, Missouri 64106

www.andrewsmcmeel.com

24 25 26 27 28 TEN 10 9 8 7 6 5 4 3 2 1

ISBN: 978-1-5248-9219-7

Library of Congress Control Number: 2023951121

Editor: Patty Rice
Art Director/Designer: Julie Barnes
Production Editor: David Shaw
Production Manager: Julie Skalla

ATTENTION: SCHOOLS AND BUSINESSES
Andrews McMeel books are available at quantity discounts with
bulk purchase for educational, business, or sales promotional use.
For information, please e-mail the Andrews McMeel Publishing
Special Sales Department: sales@amuniversal.com.

Dedicated to

Yusra, for seeing me even when
I struggle to see myself.

I

WILTING

A single flower
does not call upon spring,
but the single flower
you have plucked out of the soil and
laid in my palms
encapsulates beauty and love.
The vibrancy all our hearts hold,

until the withering.

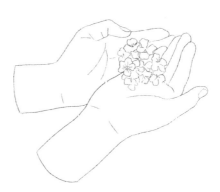

METAMORPHOSIS

I find myself grateful for the grace
which has blanketed me.
A chrysalis—after I break away from the transparent shell,
others do not recognize
the vessel of love I become.

IN SOLITUDE

We share silence
over the steam of morning tea,
coffee overflowing with creamer.

There is comfort—a refusal to change.

The cup curves around my lips.
As each day passes,
I've learned to accept your warmth.

EXISTENCE—

I have only seen its worth
encapsulated in between your arms.

If I truly understood what
love was in my youth, I surely would have
saved it only for you.

IDENTITY ISSUES

When you gaze into the mirror
I wonder what you see—
the beauty that only I notice,
or whomever you have chosen to be.

ALTERATIONS

Scenes will inevitably change,
and while that may be something
you don't look forward to,
know that it means we are allowed
to reinvent ourselves—

That we will become one with the
blossoming landscape.

ILLUMINATING

There is security
in the way your hands
clasp mine as we sit.
A need, each of your fingertips
vibrating on my skin telling me

this life would be irrelevant without
your warmth—your noor.

If this is the only thing I am worth,
my smile would never cease.

WAYFARER

Though we become lost at times,
we are wanderers. Inside, we know where to go.
But we must become those who seek—
in pursuit of themselves.
In the end, we

will always find what we are
in search of.

TARAXACUM

I've lost nights in seeking
answers that are possibly wrong.

I pretend the white speckles on my ceiling
are stars.
Looking up, I am a weed in a bed of grass.
I'd like to be a dandelion—the kind
my sisters and I would make

a wish on. Parts of me carried by breath
in each pappus.

Wherever I land

                         I am heard.

Whatever the answer may be

                         will be found.

In each heartbreak, there is clarity.
Seconds you ache to take back,
but never will—
only for it to become

what you must absorb.

Oaths

THE TRUTH

How unfair it is
that no matter what you have done,
I will always spread my arms out in forgiveness.
That if you knocked on my door and
told me your wrongdoings,

I would take you back even before you
could finish your sentence.

It was the beat of your heart
that made every day
worth living.

Oaths

Your love has taught me
how to be less afraid of believing

in myself
and in those who surround me.

MATERIALIZE

The nights where sleep refuses to soothe us,
we can't help but think of our future—
how we want our journeys' end to look like.

When, even in the darkness,
I can see your eyes widen as if you've fallen in love again,
and I want nothing more
than to make all your wishes come to fruition.

LATCH

I catch myself collapsing into the past,
where bygone sensations flare,
and so desperately desire to escape the doors
I have locked them behind.

The thought of the present
grabs hold of me.

EVERYWHERE I LOOK,

your presence hangs over my head.
Words, expressions,
even the thoughts you promised no one could hear.
And as much as I wanted you gone,

the feeling sat within me, like an anchor.
Maybe there was another chance
we could close a wound
not meant to heal.

One day. A scar.

PRAYERS

My hands cusp, interlock tightly—
even water cannot find a way through.
A whisper, as if to a lover in a crowded room
pleading—do not connect my soul to anyone

who holds impermanence.

I AM THE BEARER

There are moments where my grief refuses to become words—
instead molding itself into a stone pitted deep within me.

I am its keeper, and though it will never leave,

I will inevitably build around it.

REMORSE

I ache for my past—
how I burdened my soul
when I could have easily let myself
be untroubled.

UNSHACKLE

I am exhausted at being,
I simply desire to breathe
with my limbs unbound.

UNINVITED

I ache for you to read my story.
Every raw, unedited phrase
trapped between chapters.

I don't wish
for my past to revisit me,
a lost relative at the door
with their palms overflowing.

I'VE BEEN LYING IN THE GRASS

I hear
crows converse
through the swaying trees.
A plane howls above.

I hope
in the next life, it all makes sense.

Have I lived enough?

Perhaps I have, only in
dreams. My soul has a constant will
to wander through this world.

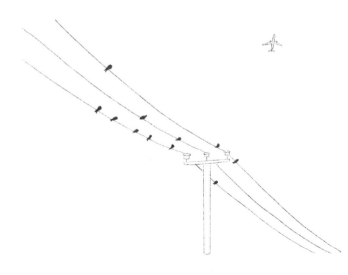

Oaths

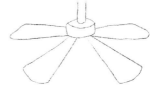

I WILL ALWAYS BE HERE

The jet-black sky,
above the pile of clothes I
have no will to organize.
The ceiling fan slowly waving.
How the hardwood floor, at times,
feels more like home.

I draw oaths on my skin—
I'd like to remember these days when
I don't want to disappear.

IN ANOTHER LIFE

I once walked past a mirror on the street.
The shattered glass,
hundreds of reflections, too many angles to grasp.
Too many me's looking at each other.

I despise the notion of parallel lives. A multiverse.

Perhaps those boys in the mirror are just like me.

DEAD SEA

Dragging a stick through the rain-soaked soil,
an extension of my body.
A boundary drawn in the midst

of struggle. I see you.
The blue sea parting with blank vacancy.

I wonder how loneliness finds life
even as your arms pull me close.
Your warmth melting my skin
as if it were ice felled beneath the summer sun.

With life, there is always a drawn breath.
Again   and   again.
Until we learn that we must
stop counting

if we are to find

                                        our will.

BRIMMING

I wonder who I am when
anger simmers. A pot boiling on the stove,
awaiting its ingredients.

Who am I
if not a person aching to be filled desperately
with anything that may quell the steam
which begs to be released?

I must search for that which will prevent me from overflowing.

DECEIVER

I have looked many in the eyes and
lied. Though badly, I have lied.
Mostly about the impregnated soil,
how the sprout had broken the surface.

How roots are left even after constantly pulling out
the stems.

How there is growth in the midst of decay.

Your smile holds keys
to doors you have yet to discover.
And behind that, only your eyes will see
all that you are worth.

How horrible
that my mind is plagued by
many irrelevant thoughts

that distract me on how I could
be focusing on you.

IN SEARCH

Everyone develops their own voice,

$\qquad$ but no one speaks of losing it.

A thief coming in when you least expect it,

$\qquad$ snatching it and leaving you directionless.

Wandering halls and rooms you visited long ago

$\qquad$ that you know do not suit you.

Old relationships resurfacing in your throat

$\qquad$ that your body is attempting to expel.

An ocean—that which does not belong

$\qquad$ cannot find home there.

My voice will be found,

$\qquad$ but first, I must search for the reasons.

IN THE NOW

There is much of this world I have not discovered,
and that thought frightens me.

That an end before my own beginning

is as capable of happening. That I will not live life
until I can only look back at it with regret.

Someone tell me
if they ever figure out a way
to live hopefully without feeling like
their world is falling in on themselves.

I will owe you my life.

SCABS

The months after you left,
every moment we had spent together
left burns on my skin.

A waste—
every word we stored in one another becoming weightless.
The love we carried peeling off my body.

SINCE YOU'VE BEEN GONE

Perhaps I feel peace,
or something too difficult to pronounce.
All I really know is that, at this very second,
I feel at one with life.
There is an ache that it is everlasting.

How could I have ever
fully loved you when parts of you
found love in hurting yourself?

Despite how heavy my past grows on me,
I will smile and laugh
as though nothing is amiss.

It will be hard to see,

but my eyes have never lied.

May I count on you
to hold me down on the days
my mind is being sporadic?

The sun has risen
through layers of clouds—
after many days of constant rain.

I hope you can stay
a bit longer this time.

The most frightening part
of letting go of the trauma
was that the good memories
lodged between my limbs

began

                    to

                              fade

                                        away too.

The person who has hurt me the most
is neither family, nor friend,

but myself.

If I am to be good for this world,

I must grow soft on my soul.

When this journey is all said and done,
I want you to know—
to really dig into yourself, to understand
that the sun was still going to rise each and every new day.
That the beauty of seasons changing
would grip you until you felt a stem
reach for the vibrant blue sky.

That this life is both defined
by what is now, and what is to come.

What we are not told
is that teachers come in forms we do not expect.

Look at those who pass—learn.

I've become exhausted of the past owning me
as if it is conjoined with the present.
Threads becoming tight-knit, like rope.
I find difficulty in cutting them loose these days.

Burn all the flowers that call
out my name. Listen to them carefully.
Who will they call to now?

Between the bruises and tears, I struggled
to see a way out.
After years of hiding in the dark, one day, I finally
opened the blinds, letting the sky take a look at me.

SUPERNOVA

Bright, dead things. I call on them
at night. Lift my finger toward the sky.

What if they see me the same way—
glimmering to the eye, yet perishing

long before they knew.

REMNANTS

The past is the past and yet, it remains.
Like broken glass on the kitchen floor,
you can't tell it's there until the blood starts to pool.

I've grown old and weary—
that's what I tell myself at least.
If I have learned one thing,
it is that what we have lived with is not a fault of ours,
but merely part of the journey.

And what we have experienced must be
fixed for the betterment of our future.

When my child asks me what I love about you,
I will think of the way you turn toward me,
our eyes meeting, and that no matter where we may be,

your smile becomes the only thing I see.

If we cared for each other genuinely,
despite what had happened between us,
we would always hope for happiness
to reach us in its own way.

I saw you today,
and for the first time in a long time
my mind didn't combust
into millions of foolish thoughts.

There are some moments when I cannot get enough
of all that you give me,
and other times when the ache is so severe
that even with all the good, you will still leave me numb.

I label my bond with life: complicated,
but as all complexity grows more understanding over time,
I am sure the differences between us will melt.
We will grow to love one another
like we were always destined to do so.

I'd like for you to have thought of me as a dream,
and with the coming of the sun, your eyes
slowly opening,

you forget.

The sun glistens like never before,
a testament that even though I see you every day,
there will always be something a little different about you.

My eyes will adjust.
I will notice more than the day before.

Oaths

When I am to die, my only hope is that
death is simple,
like closing my eyes and falling asleep
in a lover's arms.

PERSPECTIVES

I have been taught your wrath—
today, instead, I choose to believe in
the love you radiate.

II

GEMINI

May's end, my birthday. A day I can't bring myself
to love or to hate. I only yearn to
make the next year better than the last.

EXISTENCE

I sit on the dining room table under dim, warm lighting—
it is here I realize that entire lifetimes reside in between my bones.

I imagine, idealistically, life to be a linear tree. Branches reaching
in many different directions but the story leading back to the root,
attached to the trunk. Birth. A path upward.

My life is no tree—but, possibly, a plot of land. Holding many gardens
and trees that speak different dialects and
carry different shades of purple and green
and—I'd like to think—even red. I believe weeds also reside here.
The kind that grow out of cement cracks and
dandelions that children may pick up.
Trees like serpents, swimming between patches of grass
and breaking out wherever they may please.

Lifetimes. How many more gardens will come—
how many more lives will I consume before I do not need to search.

SELF-INFLICTED

I douse myself in ink until it reaches my knees,
then, my open mouth.

I ask myself why I never learned how to swim, and why
to this day, I still refuse.

Parts of me despise my parents,
other parts hold on to that which
they never wanted me to learn—
an ode to my upbringing.

Before I know it,

I'm drowning in my own voice.

RENAISSANCE

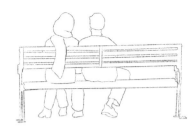

Every morning I am a witness—
if my past lives saw me now, they would refuse to believe.

Let me tell you a secret—I wasn't supposed to make it.
Many nights I didn't, the orange hues held on to me like
a mother right before I chose to never look back.

Your hands sit in my pocket today as we overlook a pond.
We walked here. Sitting on a bench and I think of how odd life is
and how I wasn't supposed to be here. I wasn't.
How if anything, I don't deserve it. This life, even
though I've paid my debts with eight years of therapy and
countless breakdowns on the closet floor over strewn clothes
and rubber bands snapping on my wrists and
how I'm fond of the feeling of my skin being cut because
that's what love was to me. I wasn't. Yet

here I am. Not yet thriving. But merely here.
In the pond, tadpoles refuse to sit still.

How life feels like it's at the end, but also, doesn't.

How even then,
one must learn to begin again.

REINCARNATION

I'd like to think that I can live every life
there is. How life is both lengthy enough
to make one choice, but not enough for two.
How I want to be everything so badly, yet
also nothing.

One day, I will (choose to) become silence.

GOLD-LADEN

Choose to see what's left of me—
I'd like you to accept me for
what I am. Broken, yet in
the process of *kintsugi*.

FAITH

I believe in a lot of things. Sometimes, too many.
Like how an apology would help
me move on, but in reality, makes me angrier
than ever.
How heaven is built for everyone, not just those
who are God-fearing.

Maybe I don't need you anymore.

How perhaps, this life was (not) made for me.

BEHIND DOORS

I wait for you to come home.

A storm passed through here while you were gone,
I didn't want to tell you.
I've picked up as much as I can so you don't see,
but this time,

I need your help.

READING

All day, I wonder how I can forget.
Move on, as if my history didn't exist.

Not realizing that my chapter now, and the ones to come,
would not make sense without the previous.

SCARCE

There are days I carry happiness,
but lately, they have become scarce—a drought.
I worry myself sick with thoughts of famine.
Looking up at the sky, waiting. Wondering
if God will come down.

Have I been abandoned by
that which I cannot live without?

DIVINITY

I have called out to you in more ways than one,
and many times, there is no response.
I wonder if that is your final answer.

There is darkness. Tall grass which hugs
my legs as the winds pass. Between my fingers,
the crease in my palms bend. I'd like to sink into
the soil sometimes. It might be worth my while.

I wonder who in this world has seen your divine nature,
and why cannot I be one you choose to show.

PATCHWORK

There are many people who I have stolen from.
A petty theft with passing conversations.
Facial expressions and
certain hand movements. And I know
copying others is wrong—I've learned that my whole life,
that plagiarism can be spotted from miles away.
My professor sitting at his desk with a magnifying glass.

But who would know the difference
if I reword a sentence,
put the end at the beginning.

Who are we if not a mosaic
of all our encounters—

We look in the mirror, seeing
stained glass with colors we don't even know the names of.

DUG UP

My father would pound the soil with his palm,
firmly, making sure that the seed would be still.
I stood behind, looking on.
Hoping to take it all in.
Hoping to take it all in.

Lately I have realized that now I am pulling
out all the roots he had a part in planting.

I would like the earth to know
that despite all that it has given me,
I ache to undo the seeds
that were planted in its soil.

To forgive—
not just those it holds

but myself

NO REARVIEW MIRRORS

There are times I question
where the path I'm on leads.
But one thing, for certain, I know—

I won't miss a soul back home.

If I have lived weeks, months,
and years without you in my life,

then I will survive.

Take me by my pain and hold me.
I'm not giving you ownership,
merely choosing you
to become part of myself.

SANCTUARY

Those whom I love,
enough for my body to stand down—
to know that it will not need to run
at a moment's notice.

For who does not crave rest?
A painless refuge from the rest of the world.

THROUGH THE CURRENTS

In nights filled with confusion and loss,
I think back to when I believed my life
to be whole. Those memories,
though I am adrift, reel me back into shore.
I take a step onto the solid ground,

knowing all will be well.

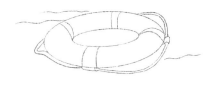

BURY

There is an ease as time passes—
the yells, cries, all words I dare not repeat.
A swirl of emotions that still makes me queasy.

There is misunderstanding, also clarity.

Before I put on my glasses in the morning,
I notice how warmly the sunlight caresses my skin.

LOOSEN

I have found that sadness desperately clings
onto the joys of my life.

That no matter how many times I loosen
its grip, it finds alternative ways to remain.

Though I have spent many years with it,
I still carry a hope that each new morning

> it will plummet.

OBTRUSION

I could never tell you
the reasons for the downfall.
Perhaps it's to teach us
that no matter how hard we try,
we will never be perfect.

Or perhaps it is to advise us
that even phases of improvements
have their interruptions.

THEY'VE BECOME ME

I may regret every mistake,
I can despise every wrongdoing
done to me and
wish they had never happened.

But I wouldn't truly be me
without every blemish.

LABYRINTH

Reasons of thread,
thin and on the verge of unwinding.
Any moment, in the blink of an eye—
I found was enough
to weave, spin into myself. A spider hidden
in the corner of every room.

And just like the cobweb one finds and rips
to shreds,
I am that which will always
be restored.

FLAWS

I often see myself in a
light no one else does, and that
seems to be my largest shortcoming.

Difficult days will end and new mornings will constantly arrive.
Pick up the pen, it is your turn to write—
use your words and build your own world.

RINSE/REPEAT

The difficulty in seeing your own worth—
when you let others place their thoughts onto you,
debris you do not need but hold on to regardless.
Its weight the one thing you begin to acknowledge even years later,
even when you've forgotten the people who spoke.

Breathe.

                Unlearn.

                                Relearn.

Rinse.

                                  Repeat.

Oaths

JOURNAL ENTRIES–FRANCE

On the train to Paris,
gazing out of the window of the train at the passing countryside,
I couldn't help but think of the past and everything I have endured.
That though all that's happened in the past wasn't entirely in my control,
it has led me here—
to these very moments with the people I love and cherish.
And even though I'm still on the journey of healing,

I find myself trying to be grateful for all of life's gifts.

HAPPENSTANCE

There are times where forgiveness refuses to come to me—
I merely grow to accept the situation
that is placed in my path

with hopes that it will liberate me.

PHOENIX

I know how difficult life has been—
how angry you've become, how
much you dump water over the fire that
refuses to go out.

Let the fire consume you,
do not repress the anger that fills you.
For the damage which comes with you may never recover.

Let your mind be its own.
Let your body crumble.

Rebirth will soon arrive
from the ashes.

GENERATIONS

Who are we if not
our ancestors' curses
attempting to find
ways to cleanse our past.

III

LOOK AT ME

A tragedy—
my heart belonging to you
as you paid no mind to it.

A childlike jealousy gripping me,
convinced that affection from only you
was the cure.

MY BODY WAS YOUR CANVAS

They say skin renews itself
every fourteen days.

I wonder why
all the tears you created
are still visible.

ONE OF THE SAME (?)

I truly wonder that since
I am made of your bones, am
I supposed to become you,

or carved out
to be the farthest thing from you?

ON DIVORCE

My father left   a flurry of words
A tornado   inevitably brings chaos and
I keep holding on to   debris / destruction

                         he left me with.

ON BOYHOOD

There are holes in me,
some the size of pennies.
Others, gaping. Large enough to fit
another body into.

I have seen him in my dreams—
the tenderness of his body,
small arms, a torso no bigger.
I feel him as though he is pocket change.

We forget how minute we once were.
An embrace enough to crush,

or to heal.

I.

I find my tears only arrive when they desire belonging—
under the scalding water,
lukewarm April rain. I stand there, clothes weighed down until
I am on my knees. Waiting.

II.

The firing squad not knowing who shot the real bullet.
The ignorant not knowing alien from American. Here, you can't tell
which droplets belong, only that they are here now.

You can't avoid them.

III.

Only that which does not exist lives within me.

KABAR

I desire nothingness, I always have.
The darkness which comes as you close your eyes,
slowly drifting into slumber. No one greeting you, no questions asked.
Even after the lowering, the tears, the dirt hugging the smooth wood.

I hope they come with me, at least. I won't
know. Well, I hope I don't.

Loneliness has always worried me, especially when I don't have
all the answers.
I hope then, when the ground rumbles and the earth becomes my
my new home,
that I am greeted by no one. Let it become
my own personal heaven.

I BLAME MYSELF

One thing about me is that I notice. I've never liked that about myself.
I see discoloring on the skin under
your long sleeve. A cut on your bottom inner lip.

How your birthmark on your left cheek
is always mistaken for lipstick

                                                    or a bruise.

Heartache is noticing all you tried to hide,
despite its happenings.

Heartache is being too insignificant to grab ahold of you.

US

My mother's feet
were once drenched in concrete—
unable to move even an inch
on her own.

The only thing we were able to do was watch.

As the years passed,
we slowly closed in on the place she stood,
hoping to aid her in escaping,
only for her to tell us
that she would rather us be free instead.

VALUE

I only wish
you had discovered the worth you hold now for me
before the day I chose to walk out of the front door.

FATHER/SON

Perhaps if we knew each other more than
the labels that were forced upon us,
we would still find ways to adore one another today.

I often think how I can still hear your laugh in mine.
Hopefully I can adore it differently than I loved you.

STREWN

When I look down, I
often find that my skin is withered
with your dying oaths.

Oaths

You adore me with your generosity
but not your voice.

And while I can tell you care about me
in your own way, my heart does not believe so.

The ocean in me is restless
and untamable.

My only desire is for you to drag me into your embrace
so these tides can finally quell.

OVERHEAR

The promises of change
never followed you home.
They would be stuck outside the door
in others' ears—

echoing through mine as if gospel.

EDGELESS

The words you speak
have begun to dull over time.
Speak till your heart is full—

I will not be pierced again.

AFTER THE CONFLICT–

Instead of it being a lesson,
you take silence as a sign of victory.

LITTLE MIRACLES

My hair tumbles out of its roots—
a fingernail chipped, broken by the strength of teeth.
A sorrow pit, planted so deep within me
that no being can dig it out,
the canary will choke before that.

Though the walls shrink as the crescents change,
I hold high in that which is minuscule.

Music shouting at me as if I am deaf.
A full moon which I stare at for so long,
a cup of coffee so rich that my soul dances with the idea of
        making another,
and another after that.

My partner leaning their head onto my shoulder.
My sister finding reason in everyday life.
The hope of my mother finally hugging me.
The ache for my father to ask for forgiveness.

Tomorrow is promised,
I plead with myself.

Tomorrow is promised.

I WANT TO BE BLOODY AND BRUISED

I just want to start it.
Throw the first punch and wait—
my arms spread out like a bird.

With every appearing bruise,
a release. Peace.

Only I know my body can be more
than what others see.

CORE MEMORIES

The friends you held close on lonely nights,
board games and coffee until the sun began peeking between the trees.
FaceTimes with the girl you fell in love with unexpectedly—
who you probably wouldn't find in another thousand lifetimes.
My parents' marriage, twenty-six years neutral,
ending in an arsonist's daydream.
So strong that even four of us could never put it out.

I've grown. Worn out, feeling a bit of a grouch.
I get the irritability that comes with age, the lack of sleep in your
        late twenties.
Feeling the depletion of my younger years that have caved in and waited
for the adult to pick them up. And not knowing where the pieces fit,
if a manual for reconstruction even exists.

I realized that it all melts, like on a hot summer day. The burning smell,
        charcoal from the grill that spills onto the redwood patio.

Ignition—we witness the burns begin to form.

(Eventually.)

DISSOCIATION

I see myself constantly,
in reflections, reaching out. My fingertips grazing
their own skin. I know history—I know mine well.

Weathered hands and a weathered mind,
my body is filled with calluses that refuse detachment.

Even after I have softened in a pool of my own tears.

SAY IT

Spit out my name,
walk on it if you must—
but first, you must say it.

1996

I'm turning twenty-seven, and I can't help but
wonder how many years you've missed out on—
how I would give up everything
just to be the prayer mat your forehead touches.
The fibers your fingers grip onto with hopes of mercy.

I'm turning twenty-seven,
and I can't help but wonder how many years
I've missed out on. On your love, years I will never get back
and moments long gone. How no matter how much
I hope, life is forever ending.

Why couldn't I be enough for you?

SURAKH

Broken like a glass slipping from a palm
on the hardwood floor, scattered beneath couches
and in crevices where you will never look
until it pierces your skin when you least expect it.

I hope you see me then,
how disastrously I was remade.

My father always said people have holes in their hands—
you better watch where you step.

MY ALTERNATE HISTORY

I'm always picking up the pieces.
Even after a decade, I still mourn.

In another life, love prospers.
Twenty-six years becomes an eternity.
Shreds are sewn as if they had never been torn.
You attempt, not only for us but for yourself.

I'm not stuck in time,
wondering the different paths I could have taken,
that all love ends one way or another.

That perhaps, my life was meant to be lived alone.

WHEN I CAN'T SLEEP

Listen, I enjoy torturing myself.
Asking myself questions that are swallowed before
they are answered like,

Why

I wasn't enough for you to stay?
did you hate me since the day I left the slit in her stomach?
you saw me like you saw your own reflection?
at the kitchen table in fifth grade,
       my neck was wrung like a towel?
prayer never made sense since you were the one leading?
does heaven exist if you believe you'll be there?
pain feels like a childhood friend?
like you, I still bite my nails till the blood comes?
home has never felt like home and I keep wandering?
I don't feel, but know, that I will end life alone?
no one truly loves me?
it feels like everyone will leave their knives in me?
I can't cut myself open to those I love anymore?
years of life have lost their meaning?

can't I forget.

115

I HEAR YOU WHEN I SPEAK

I have your smile but not your eyes.
Sometimes I wish I did—perhaps seeing the world
the way you did would've made me know.

Your laugh still sits in the back of my throat like
bedrock. The one I always heard but could
never pull out. No matter how hard I tugged,
my skin ripped at the seams.

YOU LIVE WITH ME, STILL

I stay up late and wonder how bonds
have made us who we are.

How I wish home was your arms so I wouldn't keep on searching.

That we don't choose, but are forced to love and remember.

If you came to the door knocking for forgiveness, I'd yield.

How I wish, ache, we could have gotten to know each other
for who we were, not who we wanted each other to be.

Every time my forehead touches the ground.

All I think of is you.

No matter how hard I try to forget

I can't.

SPROUTING

The last couple months, I have been reflecting. In the mirrors as I enter new rooms, noticing longer hair, fuller cheeks, darker eyes. My first memory at the bottom of the stairs, asking my father

How old am I?

Him saying

Three.

The way I learned Arabic letters before the English alphabet, my fingers tracing long verses, a childhood friend which I've grown apart from. My brothers who do not share my blood but know me more than those who do, why they have never been able to see my cracked skin, why I have never been able to see theirs. My mother burying the woman she was, vandalizing pictures of her younger self, becoming a person I hope I can learn to love someday. My nephew looking at baby pictures of my siblings and I, pointing to a kid I vaguely recognize, saying that he wants to be just like him.

I WANT TO BE A WITNESS

The only thing I've ever desired in this life
is for you to have an ache to want me. Desperately.
As if I'm the air that fills your lungs. I want to see
the scratch marks on your throat. The blood in your eyes
as they bulge. I want to be the sole reason.

I don't want you to tell me—I want to see it with
my own two eyes.

BROKEN CONCRETE

My mother tells me how she is in love. I notice the air
and how it seems thin around her. In the clouds and
simply living. My wife teases her, and my mother
asks how she can send a message to him. How if she was with
him when she was younger, he would never have gotten divorced.
How no one in the world could compete against the love she can give.

The house has become calm ever
since my younger sister moved out. A sunrise. It's all quiet and
you take in a breath of fresh morning dew.
This time I can't tell if it's good or bad. Only simple.
I've never seen her smile
this much. How it took five of us leaving for her to live without
worry.

I adore it—over and over again, I would do it for her to be free.

MY MIND WANDERS

At a nightclub in Montreal. I saw
unraveling. I don't dance. I never liked to.
My body moves like a tree on a breezeless summer day.

I remember running. I think of religion. Of God.
How all of where I stand is creation. Made by hands,

who made those fingers?

                        Passion. The rope tightens.

How love is not love until you spit on it. Dance over it.
Call it names until the seas part.   Until you come back.

                        How did they meet?
                The couple kissing in the corner.

In the darkness

                        you notice beauty.

I'M GRIEVING

Over the unlit fireflies in the jar we forgot to poke holes through.
Do you know how many years we've lost on bickering? I counted,
it's been ten years since Mama and Papa started fighting (seven
since the divorce was finalized). Since then, we've focused on
only ourselves, and I can't fault anyone for that because we were
only trying to survive. Emotional hunger, motion sickness. And
none of us had realized we were starving until the wrong people
fed us, and now we stare at each other and wonder why we
struggle to breathe, why someone forgot to poke holes in the lid,
and why we cannot hum in the dark. Until now, when every day
has become the same and I ache to have the warmth we never
did, and I've realized I'm grieving, still. Over the light that will
only live if we let it.

Oaths

CRAVINGS

Many years have passed,
I constantly question where we stand.

Your silence is excruciating.
The skin wrapped around you
coated in thorns.

There are moments your embrace is so tight
that there is no room for air—
I could die peacefully.

CITRUS

Nails dig into orange peels
the way they were dug into my skin.

The sun is above, your hands cupped in prayer,
I still think of that tear that fell from your

eyes. You do not see all
that you have done, only because

you refuse acceptance. You believe you were sculpted
the way it was intended. The world smiles

in my dreams. I am who I want to be.
Until I wake—

your memory greeting me.

FORESIGHT

Markings on my skin.
Fingerprints, from when hands would wrap around me.
Yellow stains of cigarette smoke, my head resting at the
side of your open car window, inhaling your exhale.
People are disgusted when I say I love the smell,
how I truly can't get enough of it some days, even though
I have never taken a drag myself.

My skin is filled with your dying dreams.
Your eyes might've seen it the day I was birthed.

REGRETS

I believed that you were immortal.

You had time, that's what I told myself at least.
I never gave you the warmth you desired
in the days you had left.

ACKNOWLEDGMENTS

When it comes to *Oaths*, I want to firstly acknowledge everyone who's seen me. I spent most of my childhood invisible, but every day I'm trying to find myself. And my readers are the first ones who made me feel seen. I'm forever grateful for that.

Mama, for being one of the strongest women I know. I'm sorry I never realized earlier that you struggled too. I love you more than you know, even if I struggle showing it from time to time.

Yusra, my love. There's a lot I'd like to say to you, but it could make up another book. I hope I can always keep on writing it. Thank you for always being someone I can bounce synonyms off of, and a person who's very honest about my work. You always make me want to be better, not only for you but for myself. (Also for Stormi and Yuki.)

Aqsa, Nida, Eiman, Ibbu, Yunus, Ayubi, Aya, and Hana. Family wouldn't be family without you guys. I can't lie, I'm so excited for what our futures will look like. Hope we can keep on growing together. Now and always.

Waqar, Nusrat, Sania, Shayan, Wisam, Safa, Musa, and Mina. I never felt like I was deserving of family until you all made me your own.

Imam, Osama, Shy, and Taaha for being some of my greatest friends, appeasing my very unhealthy board game addiction (and constantly beating me at games I teach you guys) and being people I can shut my overthinking brain around. I wouldn't be me without you all.

Sara Bawany, for being my writing-buddy-rock and a person I will forever trust with my work first and foremost. Thank you for editing *Oaths*, especially with the time crunch. It wouldn't have been what it is without you. You brought the best out of me, and I hope I can return the favor someday.

Trinity and James, for being the best agents and believing in me as a writer. Whenever you two spoke to me, I always felt at ease and believed in myself a little more than before. My career would be nowhere without you two.

Patty Rice and Andrews McMeel for believing in my work and knowing I have more to tell. Thank you for giving *Oaths* a home.

And lastly, Papa.

Thank you for failing to make me just like you.

INDEX